W9-CKI-223

Heroes and Villains of the

WILD WEST

Billy the Kid

by John Hamilton

ABDO & Daughters
PUBLISHING

Published by Abdo & Daughters, 4940 Viking Dr., Suite 622, Edina, MN 55435.

Cover Photo by: Archive Photos
Inside Photos by:
Bettmann Archive: pp. 15, 23, 27
Wide World Photos: p. 13
Archive Photos: pp. 9, 17, 19

Edited by Ken Berg

Library of Congress Cataloging–in–Publication Data
Hamilton, John, 1959–
    Billy the Kid / by John Hamilton
        p. cm. — (Heroes & villains of the wild West)
    Includes bibliographical references and index.
    Summary: The life story of Billy the Kid, the outlaw of the Old West, from his childhood and participation in the Lincoln County Range War to his death at the hands of Pat Garrett.
    ISBN: 1-56239-558-0
    1. Billy, the Kid—Juvenile literature. 2. Outlaws—Southwest, New — Biography—Juvenile literature. 3. Southwest, New—Biography— Juvenile literature. [1. Billy, the Kid. 2. Robbers and outlaws. 3. Southwest, New—History—1848–] I. Title. II. Series.
    F786.B4H35 1996
    364.1'552'092—dc20   95-25041
    [B]   CIP
                                                                                     AC

Contents

Henry McCarty

Few outlaws of the Wild West have had more information, or misinformation, spread about them than the notorious Billy the Kid. Some call him a western Robin Hood who stood for justice and loyalty, stealing from the rich to give to the poor. Others brand him a low-down thief, liar, and murderer, no better than the worst criminal. The truth is probably somewhere between. In any case, Billy the Kid died young, his candle snuffed out before he could enjoy the fame he so craved.

His real name was Henry McCarty. He was born in the slums of New York City on September 17, 1859, to William Bonney and Catherine McCarty. After his father died near the end of the Civil War, his mother resumed her maiden name, McCarty, and moved the family (herself, Henry, and his older brother Joseph) out West. They finally settled in lawless Silver City, in the New Mexico Territory. There she married William Antrim, who earned a living as a miner.

Up to this point, Henry was no better or worse than any other boy growing up in the dirt-lined streets of a frontier town. He was rowdy, but so were many of the boys his age. In fact, he once was employed by a local hotel. The owner remarked that Henry was "the only kid who ever worked here who never stole anything."

Billy the Kid.

Turning to a Life of Crime

In 1874, when young Henry was just 15, his mother died of tuberculosis, or what was known back then as "consumption." Henry's stepfather did the best he could for the two boys. But he was often gone prospecting for gold for long periods of time. Henry's older brother did alright, eventually settling down in Denver. Henry, however, mixed in with a rowdy group of boys and was quickly up to no good.

His first known offense was at age 16. An older boy convinced Henry to hide some stolen laundry. Henry was caught holding the bag and thrown into prison to teach him a lesson. The crime was detailed in the Grant County Herald on September 26, 1875: "Henry McCarty, who was arrested on Thursday and committed to the jail to await the action of the Grand Jury upon the charge of stealing clothes from Charley Sun and Sam Chung... escaped from prison yesterday through the chimney. It's believed that Henry was the simple tool of 'Sombrero Jack,' who done the stealing whilst Henry done the hiding. Jack has skinned out."

After fleeing jail by climbing out the chimney, Henry blew out of town and began the life of a drifter, working odd jobs from ranch to ranch. Life was hard, dull, and lonely. It made the young man sullen and mean. Crime became inviting.

By 1877, Henry had drifted to Arizona Territory and was working at a sawmill at the Camp Grant army post. It was here that Henry got his nickname, "the Kid." (It was here also that he changed his last name to Bonney, after his father. He also changed his first name to William, or Billy, after his stepfather.) He had a slender build, being barely 5 feet 8 inches tall, and about 140 pounds. His light hair and blue eyes made him

appear younger than he really was. Though he seemed good-natured, fun-loving, and had a disarming smile, Billy was sensitive of his small size and hated being picked on.

A blacksmith named Frank "Windy" Cahill liked poking fun at the wiry young lad. One day he made the mistake of calling Billy a discouraging word. Billy returned with a curse of his own, and a fight began. During the brawl, Billy drew his Colt six-shooter and nailed Cahill stone-cold dead. Billy was arrested for murder, but escaped once again. He stole a horse and high-tailed it to Mesilla, New Mexico, where he hid until the heat was off. Now, however, he was a killer.

The Lincoln County Range War

Billy drifted around from ranch to ranch, earning a reputation as a gambler and quick-draw. He also was a practical joker, with humor that was rough even for the Wild West. Sometimes he liked to sit laughing as he tossed bullets into the campfire and watched his friends go scurrying for cover. He also discovered that, for him, crime often paid better than an honest day's work.

After a couple of months rustling horses, Billy moved north to Lincoln County, where he became involved in the bloody Lincoln County Range War. The "war" was actually a clash between cattle barons (owners of huge livestock herds) who controlled much of the business in the area, and a group of men who fought for the right to go into business for themselves. Billy drifted to the ranch of Englishman John Tunstall, where he got a job as a ranch hand.

Tunstall was an eager young man who sought to invest in ranching and a general store in the town of Lincoln. Unfortunately, Lawrence G. Murphy & Company, a powerful ranching and general merchandise organization, already owned nearly everything in the area. They didn't take kindly to the uppity Englishman moving in on their turf. Since the law had little power in Lincoln County, the stage was set for violence.

Billy took a liking to John Tunstall. It's said that a bond developed between the young drifter and the cultured and kind-hearted Englishman, and that Billy was extremely loyal to his employer. "That's the finest lad I ever met," Tunstall once said. "He's a revelation to me every day and would do anything on earth to please me. I'm going to make a man of that boy yet."

Tunstall didn't get much of a chance to keep his word. On February 18, 1878, a posse hired by the Murphy Company, and deputized by Sheriff

A Southwestern cattle ranch.

William Brady, caught Tunstall on a lonely road and murdered him in cold blood. Billy and several other ranch hands witnessed the killing. Billy was outraged and vowed revenge. The Lincoln County Range War had turned bloody.

Alexander McSween had been John Tunstall's partner. As a lawyer, McSween was able to get warrants for the arrest of the thugs responsible for Tunstall's murder. However, Murphy (of Murphy Company) was a good friend of the governor, and arranged the firing of the justice of the peace who had issued the warrants. The warrants were then declared useless.

Frustrated, but still wanting revenge against the murderers, McSween took action anyway. Since the law, including Sheriff Brady, was on the side of the Murphy Company, McSween gave responsibility of the murderers' arrest to his foreman, Dick Brewer, and a posse of some 10 men. They called themselves the "Regulators," and Billy the Kid was a part of this posse. Roaring mad, he was ready for blood.

On March 9, two of the outlaws, Bill Morton and Frank Baker, were taken captive. Billy wanted to kill them right away, but Brewer said no. They were still trying to act within the law, despite the rampant corruption in Lincoln County. Two days later, however, the unarmed prisoners were "shot attempting to escape." It was obviously a gang-style killing, though, since each corpse held 11 bullets.

On April 1, Sheriff Brady and three deputies were walking down Lincoln's main street. Suddenly, shots erupted from behind a gate. Sheriff Brady was killed instantly, struck in the back several times. Billy stepped out, guns blazing at the other men. He snatched the Sheriff's new Winchester rifle and then quickly rode out of town.

The ambush outraged most folks in Lincoln County, swinging opinion against the Regulators. After several skirmishes, including one in which Dick Brewer was shot dead through the eye, Billy found himself leading the remaining Regulators in a losing struggle against the corrupt cattle barons. Finally, in mid-July, the war came to a head.

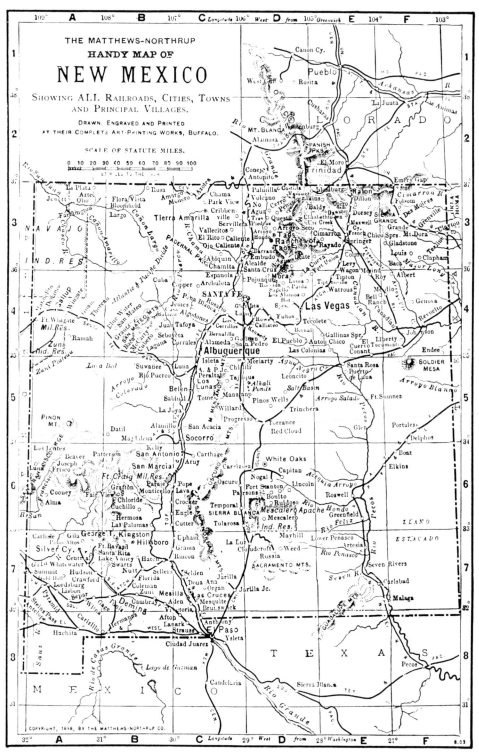

An old map of New Mexico in 1898.

11

Billy and about 25 other armed men had holed up in lawyer McSween's house in the middle of Lincoln. After a five-day standoff that eventually involved the U.S. Army surrounding the house, McSween and several others were killed. The house in flames, Billy escaped under cover of darkness. The Lincoln County War was at an end.

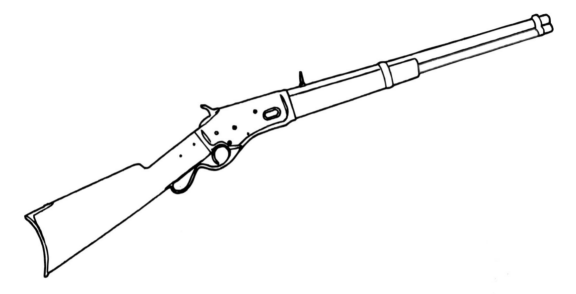

A Whitney-Kennedy lever-action .44-40 caliber carbine used by Billy the Kid. Billy gave the rifle to Deputy U.S. Marshal Eugene Van Patten for the fair treatment he was given while in custody. Today the rifle is on display at the Gene Autry Western Heritage Museum in Los Angeles, California.

WILLIAM BONNEY. BILLY THE KID
An illustration of a young Billy the Kid.

Lawlessness

Although the range war was over—with Tunstall and McSween dead and Billy the Kid on the run—lawlessness still terrorized the countryside. Billy collected some of the one-time Regulators and others, taking up cattle rustling and murdering anyone who tried to stop them. Tension got so bad that settlers began leaving the territory, afraid for their lives. The Kid also began horse stealing, driving them to the Texas Panhandle and selling them. Billy's profits were usually spent gambling at his new base, Fort Sumner, in New Mexico. There he met a likable bartender named Pat Garrett, a former buffalo hunter from Texas.

Too many ranchers were dying defending their herds against Billy and his gang of outlaws. The new governor, General Lew Wallace, had to take action. His first move was to grant amnesty to anyone involved in the Lincoln County War. If the citizens who had participated would come in peacefully, the law would leave them alone. Billy the Kid, however, was not included in the offer. He was still wanted for the cold-blooded murder of Sheriff Brady. The governor offered a $500 reward for the capture of the Kid. People were so sick and fed up with the lawlessness that the reward was soon raised to $1,000. Billy the Kid was only 19.

Billy formed a new gang, which was comprised of old Regulator riders and cattle rustlers. Among them were friends Charlie Bowdre and Tom O'Folliard. Together they began rustling livestock from the cattle barons, which made them hopping mad. Other old enemies in the range war were still killing each other left and right. Billy was an eyewitness to one murder, that of a lawyer named Huston Chapman. Wanting to give society a second chance, the Kid contacted Governor Wallace and made him a deal: Billy would testify against Chapman's killers in exchange for a pardon. (He claimed he hadn't given up much earlier because he was afraid his enemies would kill him, which seems likely considering how many people Billy had wronged.) The governor agreed, and Billy surrendered. Several days passed in prison, however, with no word from

A woodcut illustration showing Billy the Kid gunning down a foe who had taken refuge behind a saloon bar. First published in "Illustrated Police News" in 1884.

the governor. Billy began to worry, suspicious that Governor Wallace was going to double-cross him. So, yet again, Billy broke out of prison, this time by slipping the handcuffs off his skinny wrists and walking away.

So, Billy and his gang started all over still again, terrorizing the Territory and rustling horses and cattle for over a year and a half. A bounty hunter may have been hired to get the Kid, but the plan backfired. Instead, the Kid laid the bounty hunter to rest six feet under, riddled with lead. It was the last straw for Governor Wallace. Billy the Kid had to be captured, dead or alive!

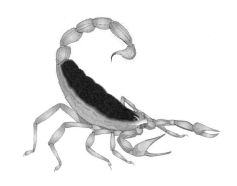

A wanted poster offering a reward of $5,000 for the capture of Billy the Kid, dead or alive.

Captured!

In November of 1880, Pat Garrett, the former buffalo hunter and bartender, was elected sheriff of Lincoln County. He was a brave man, a crack shot, and knew the countryside well. Standing 6 feet 4 inches, the burly Garrett was feared by most outlaws. The feuding between the cattle barons had mostly died out by this time. The biggest remaining obstacle to peace in the Territory was Billy the Kid. Garrett knew Billy and his habits well, having befriended the Kid while in Fort Sumner. Garrett felt sure he could capture Billy, and began his hunt almost from the moment he became sheriff.

Billy and his men had been holing up in various places near Fort Sumner. Garrett, through the use of spies, knew that one of Billy's pals, Charlie Bowdre, had a wife living at the fort. Garrett was confident that if he waited long enough, Billy and his gang would eventually show up. Bowdre's wife was housed in an old hospital building on the edge of the fort. Knowing the gang would come in that direction, Garrett and his force waited.

One snowy December evening, in the dead of night, Garrett and his men were passing the time playing cards. Suddenly, a guard called into the room, "Pat, someone is coming!"

Garrett reached for his weapons and stepped for the door. "Get your guns, boys," he said. "No one but the men we want would be riding at this time of night."

Billy had been riding at the front of his party, headed straight for Fort Sumner. As they drew closer, however, a sense of danger overcame the Kid. As he later told Pat Garrett, "I wanted a chew of tobacco bad. Somebody had some in the rear. I went back after tobacco, don't you see?" he said with mischief. Whatever the reason, by the time the gang reached the front porch of the old hospital, Billy's friend Tom O'Folliard was riding in front. Garrett and one of his deputies, a man called Chambers, stepped

Sheriff Pat Garrett.

19

out of the shadows. "Halt!" shouted Garrett. It was then that the shooting started.

"When I called 'Halt!'" Garrett later wrote, "O'Folliard reached for his pistol, but before he could draw it, Chambers and I both fired. His horse wheeled and ran at least a hundred and fifty yards. As quick as possible I fired at Pickett (another of Billy's men), but the flash of Chambers' gun disconcerted my aim, and I missed him. But one might have thought by the way he ran and yelled that I had a dozen bullets in him. When O'Folliard's horse ran with him, he was uttering cries of mortal agony; and we were convinced that he had received a death wound. But he wheeled his horse, and as he rode slowly back, said, "Don't shoot, Garrett. I am killed." O'Folliard soon took his last breath and bit the dust.

Billy and the remainder of the gang high-tailed it to the countryside, but they left tracks in the fresh snow. It wasn't long before Garrett and his men were hot on their trail. They followed the gang for several days, getting leads from local ranchers. Finally, the lawmen tracked the desperadoes to an old stone house in a place called Stinking Springs, east of Fort Sumner. It was night when they surrounded the house. Several horses were tethered up outside. Garrett decided to wait until dawn to make his move. His plan was to kill Billy and hope that the others, their leader dead, would give up readily.

When the sun cracked over the horizon, a man came out of the house and walked toward the horses with a feed bag in his hand. The man looked like the Kid, and wore the same kind of hat Billy preferred. Garrett and his group opened up with Winchester rifles, muzzle flames blazing in the dim morning light. The man went down and desperately crawled for the doorway. But the lawmen had shot the wrong man, Charlie Bowdre, not Billy. Garrett shouted for the men inside to give themselves up.

Inside the house, Billy took one look at the mortally wounded Bowdre and drew his revolver, slapping it into the dying man's hand. "They have murdered you, Charlie," he said, "but you can get revenge. Kill some of (them) before you die." Bowdre staggered out of the house with the gun in his hand but his arms in the air. He managed to totter up to Garrett

The capture of Billy the Kid by Sheriff Pat Garrett and his posse at Stinking Springs, New Mexico. Part of an illustration from Garrett's book, *The Authentic Life of Billy the Kid*.

before collapsing. Nearly dead, Bowdre croaked out, "I wish— I wish— I wish. . ." Then he clutched his chest. "I am dying!" Shot near the heart, Bowdre never stirred again.

Meanwhile, Billy managed to move a horse inside the windowless stone house and was trying to make a grab for the rest tethered outside. Not wanting the gang to mount and get a running start out the door, Garrett shot one of the horses. It fell dead, blocking the doorway. The lawman then shot the ropes holding the remaining horses, which galloped away. Escape was now impossible, and Billy and his men were left with no food or water. After a time, Sheriff Garrett kindled a fire and began frying food over a hot griddle. It was too much for the hungry outlaws to take, and they reluctantly surrendered. Garrett slapped leg irons on the prisoners and transported them back for trial. Billy was convicted of the murder of Sheriff Brady and sentenced to be hanged in Lincoln. He was driven there and held at the local jail.

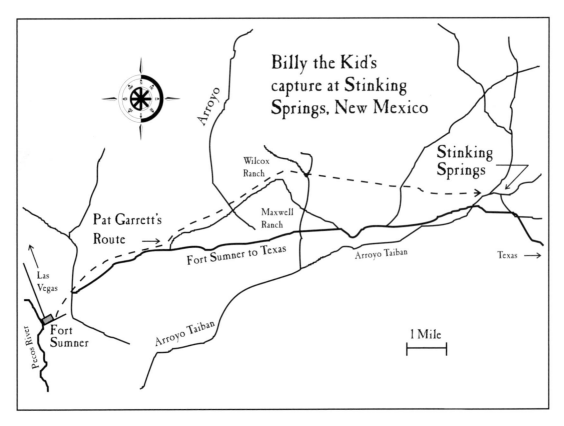

Billy the Kid's capture at Stinking Springs, New Mexico

Sheriff Pat Garrett bringing in Billy the Kid and his gang.

Billy's Last Days

On April 28, 1881, days before he was due to be hanged, Billy broke out from behind bars yet again. This time, with a pistol secretly snuck into prison by persons unknown, he slew his two guards. He rode off on a stolen horse, but not before making fools of everybody in town. Said one report, "The Kid was all over the building, on the porch, watching from the windows. He danced about the balcony, laughed and shouted as though he had not a care on earth."

Sheriff Garrett was called back to duty and relentlessly picked up the Kid's trail once more. Incredibly, Billy wandered back to his old haunts at Fort Sumner. Garrett received a tip that Billy was staying with a friend, sheep rancher Pete Maxwell, who had a large house with guest rooms at the fort. On July 14, 1881, Garrett and two deputies hid themselves near the "Maxwell House" and waited. After midnight, Garrett slipped into Pete Maxwell's room, surprising Billy's friend. Warning the sheep rancher to keep quiet, Garrett started questioning him about the whereabouts of the Kid. Garrett's deputies waited outside.

Meanwhile, Billy was returning from a dance in search of a midnight snack. At the time he was carrying a long hunting knife and his favored weapon, a Colt .41 caliber double-action "Thunderer" pistol. Suddenly, Billy spotted the two deputies lurking in the shadows. Suspicious, he slipped into Maxwell's room to find out if his friend knew what was happening. Garrett sat waiting for him, his Colt .45 cocked and ready.

Billy heard someone breathing in the darkened room. "Pete, who are they?" Billy whispered. "Quien es? (Who is it?)" Without a word of warning, Garrett opened fire, his gun roaring in the tiny room. The lawman's first shot struck Billy in the chest, just above the heart. The Kid's lifeless body slumped to the floor. Soon the deputies outside saw Garrett run from the room, shouting, "I killed the Kid! I killed the Kid!" After a few moments, the trembling sheriff went back inside the room,

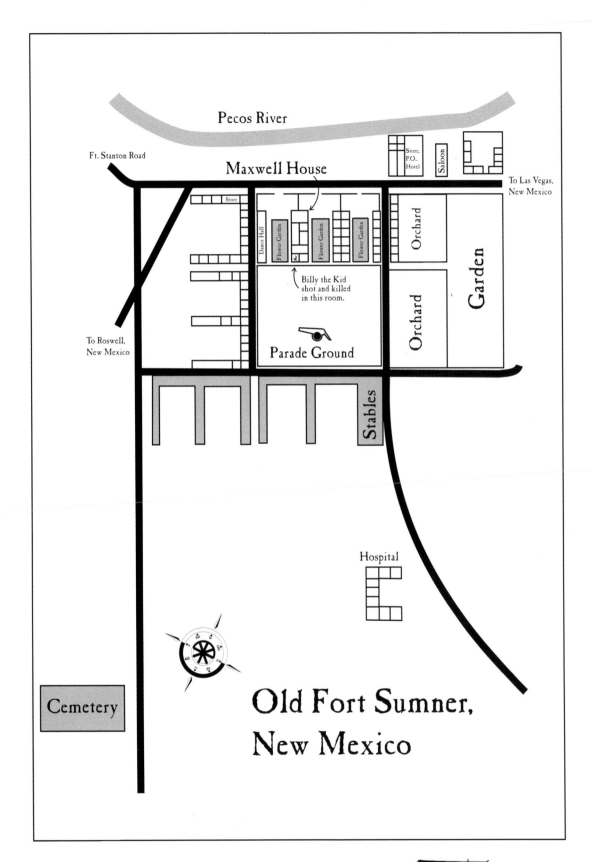

Pecos River

Ft. Stanton Road

Maxwell House

Store, P.O., Hotel

Saloon

To Las Vegas, New Mexico

Store

Dance Hall

Flower Garden

Flower Garden

Flower Garden

Orchard

Garden

Billy the Kid shot and killed in this room.

To Roswell, New Mexico

Parade Ground

Orchard

Stables

Hospital

Cemetery

Old Fort Sumner, New Mexico

where he saw Pete Maxwell's wife, Deluvina, cradling Billy's body in her arms. She looked up at Garrett. "You didn't have the nerve to kill him face to face," she sneered.

Many people thought Garrett was a cowardly murderer for the way in which he killed Billy the Kid. But a coroner's jury decided that the killing was "justifiable homicide." As Garrett would later write, ". . . he came there armed with a pistol and knife expressly to kill me if he could . . . I had no alternative but to kill him, or suffer death at his hands."

Today Billy is buried at Fort Sumner Cemetery. His remains lie between two of his old pals, gang members Tom O'Folliard and Charlie Bowdre. As for Garrett, the lawman lived a rocky life until, in 1908, he was murdered, shot in the back with his own shotgun.

Billy the Kid was just 21 when he died. By all accounts he was a savage, mean-tempered hoodlum who wouldn't think twice about gunning a man down if it served his purposes. Yet history has taken a shine to Billy. Within a year after his death, at least 10 books were written about him, including Sheriff Garrett's *An Authentic Life of Billy the Kid*. Many took delight in glorifying his bloody deeds. Some insisted that he killed a man for each of his 21 years, but that's hardly true. Why such an interest in a low-down wretch like the Kid? Perhaps it was his youth, or a human desire to cheer for the underdog. Whatever the reason, in 1881 Billy the Kid died, but his legend had just begun.

Billy the Kid killed by Sheriff Pat Garrett at Fort Sumner, New Mexico.

The Wild West of Billy the Kid

New Mexico

Fort Sumner

Lincoln County

Stinking Springs

Lincoln •

• Silver City

• Mesilla

Glossary

amnesty

A general pardon for criminals or offenders by a government.

bounty hunter

Someone who hunts criminals or outlaws for money.

cattle baron

A person who, honestly or by twisting the law, becomes the owner of huge sections of rangeland and has his brand on a large herd of cattle. The term was usually meant as a sort of insult, but many honest and well-respected men were referred to as cattle barons.

Civil War

The war fought in the United States between Union forces (the North) and the Confederacy (the South), between 1861 and 1865. The dispute over whether or not people should own slaves was a major cause of the war.

Colt

A type of pistol commonly used in the Old West. The full tradename is Colt's Revolver. It was developed by Samuel Colt (1814-1862), American inventor and manufacturer of firearms. The Colt was a practical and reliable weapon, and was in great demand in the West and other parts of the country. Anyone who could pull a trigger could now defend themselves in the many lawless regions of the West. A popular saying at the time was, "God created man, but Sam Colt made them equal!"

posse

A group of citizens who are given legal authority to round up criminals.

rustling

To steal cattle. As opposed to "mavericking," a legal activity where unbranded cattle on the open range are rounded up and added to a rancher's herd. Stealing cattle already marked with another rancher's brand was a serious crime in the Old West. Cattle thieves were often shot or hanged.

shotgun

A shoulder-held firearm that shoots steel or lead pellets through a smooth bore. Commonly used in hunting birds. Shotguns are also sometimes preferred by lawmen and robbers because they are powerful weapons with a wide blast area, making it easier to hit a moving target than with a pistol, especially at close range.

tuberculosis

A contagious disease that usually causes lesions, or sores, in the lungs of humans. Antibiotics have made tuberculosis much less common than it was at the turn of the century.

Winchester

A very popular type of rifle in the Old West, especially the legendary Model of 1873. Billy the Kid used a variety of Winchester rifles during his career in crime.

Bibliography

Earle, James H., (Ed.). *The Capture of Billy the Kid.* College Station, TX: Creative Publishing Company, 1988.

Flanagan, Mike. *Out West.* New York: Harry N. Abrams, Inc., 1987.

Garrett, Pat F. *The Authentic Life of Billy the Kid.* Santa Fe: New Mexico Printing and Publishing Company, 1882.

Nash, Jay Robert. *Bloodletters and Badmen.* New York: M. Evans and Company, 1973.

Rosa, Joseph G. *Age of the Gunfighter.* New York: Smithmark Publishers, Inc., 1993.

Steckmesser, Kent Ladd. *Western Outlaws.* Claremont, California: Regina Books, 1985.

Ulyatt, Kenneth. *Outlaws.* Philadelphia and New York: J.B. Lippincott Company, 1976.

Wallechinsky, David, and Wallace, Irving, (Ed.). *The People's Almanac #2.* New York: Bantam Books, 1978.

Index